Synaptic Impulses

Synaptic Impulses

Reflection through Prose and Poetry

Abrar Ansari

Abstract Space Inc

Dedicated to the one who has provided me with an abode of tranquility with her love and companionship, my wife, Vaseem Ansari.

Copyright © 2010, 2022 by Abrar Ansari

All rights reserved. No part of this book may be reproduced in any manner whatsoever without written permission except in the case of brief quotations embodied in critical articles and reviews.

Second Printing, 2022
ISBN # 978-1-7357678-3-3

Published by:
Abstract Space Inc.

First published by:
SAMA
Editorial and Publishing Services
Karachi, Pakistan 2010
ISBN 978-969-8784-69-0 (Hardbound)

CONTENTS

DEDICATION iv

Why A Second Edition?

Acknowledgements

Preface

1 Companionship 7

Relationships 9

Ripple Effect 10

Coming Together 11

Inner Connection 12

Grace 13

Destiny's Whisper 14

CONTENTS

2 | Collisions   15

What I Know Now   17

Neglect   18

Superficialities   19

Metamorphosis   20

The Transcendence   21

A Fleeting Moment   22

3 | Cobwebs   23

Inner Turmoil   24

The Toll   25

Forgotten Promises   26

My Creed   27

Human Suffering   28

Agitation   29

Inner Folds   30

CONTENTS

4	Souls	31
	A Soul's Journey	32
	Signs	33
	The Drowning	34
	Hope	35
	Compassion	36
	Due Drops	37
5	Affairs	38
	Eye of Desire	40
	Dichotomy	41
	A Land of Not So Free	42
	Unconscious Erosion	43
	Humble Stare	44
	The Abyss	45
6	Thoughts	46

CONTENTS

I Swear 47

Out in the Open 48

Slow Trickles 49

Your Awareness 50

7 | Oaths 51

Promises 53

Getting By 54

Good Deeds 55

Our Backdoor 56

8 | Consciousness 57

Cancer 59

Words 60

Salesman 61

Beckoning 62

The Coming of Age 63

CONTENTS

9 | Interdependencies 65

Who Am I? 66

Connectivity 67

Mother 68

10 | Destiny 69

Sublime Contemplation 70

One Droplet at a Time 71

Smile 72

ABOUT THE AUTHOR 73

Why A Second Edition?

The last couple of years, a shift in my priorities has allowed me to focus more on my writing. That change has given me the opportunity to recently published a book on management. Now that I'm done with that book, I am focusing my attention on poetry.

Since a very limited hard cover first edition of Synaptic Impulses was published in 2010 in Pakistan, my reach to a global audience was limited. Over the years, I have had quite a few requests from people to get the book reprinted.

The perils we face today— from the polarization of thought and numbness towards suffering, to the total disregard of human dignity, to rise in extreme inequity, resource scarcity, climate change, waste and pollution, and last but-not-least destruction of ecosystems and the loss of biodiversity —require deep introspection on our part. We all need to do our part in preventing harm and promoting good in this world we live in; a commitment that requires us to rethink what preservation of Life, Dignity, Reason, Wealth, and the Future means to us. (topic of my book, entitled Management by Intent, the Five Principles).

Over the last decade, I have written a steady stream of poems to express my feeling on these topics. But the number of these poems are not enough to warrant a second book. So, for this second addition, I am adding about a dozen new ones with the old.

Acknowledgements

I acknowledge that infinite blessings and mercy have perpetually come my way only because of the will of my Creator, the Lord of all realms, the Cherisher, the Sustainer.

Every individual, whom I have run into in the course of my life, has helped shape my thoughts and my actions in some way or the other. I am indebted to all those who came into my life, for better or for worse, for influencing me to be who I am today.

I am eternally grateful to my parents for their relentless efforts in shaping my character and instilling in me many virtues that have become part of my personality. I acknowledge my siblings, my family, and my friends for believing in my talent and building my confidence over the years by providing me with opportunities to write and express myself.

Preface

All human beings are endowed with certain capabilities that are God given and innate to our souls. What we do with these capabilities in this life is up to us. We will be held accountable for them one day! Once we understand that accountability in our everyday living, we go through a spiritual awakening.

We all go through awakenings at various stages of our lives; awakenings that shape our physical, mental and spiritual realms. Most of us are very familiar with physical awakenings. Ask any adult about their entering adolescence and you'll be surprised how many will very quickly recall episodes of physical awakenings in their life; all associated to their lower base desires.

Physical awakenings play a critical role in helping us adapt to the material world around us. How many times little kids come to us asking us to tickle them. The enjoyment they get from being tickled is a physical awakening of certain sensory receptors in them. The sensation is addictive at that stage as it opens up new emotional doors for them. When was the last time a grownup asked you to tickle them?

Physical awakenings are the easiest paradigm shifts to go through. Most of the time, recovery is not required, and experiences are stimulating. People learn new things and rapidly adapt. Physical awakenings can be addictive and hence require discipline to control.

Next are mental paradigm shifts; awakenings that shape our internal reasoning mechanism. That's a tough one for most people. Having a mental image of something shattered within you leaves deep scars; scars that sometimes only time heals. Recovery is required! Some people can never recover from such a traumatic shift.

Life is just so full of physical and mental awakenings that seldom do people find the time for a spiritual awakening. Unlike the other two, spiritual awakening takes a concerted effort, an active realization on the part of the individual trying to seek one. You can't willy-nilly hop on the 'spiritual high' bandwagon. That journey starts off with an inward reflection of one's self.

This short book of poems is about my inward journey; my attempt to decipher the meaning of my life. My hope is that whoever reads it reflects upon their inner journey inculcating a desire to change for the better, rather than just cluttering their minds with yet another set of readings.

May we all continue to read and learn new things in life that are beneficial to us and others around us. And may we, from the wisdom that we are given, continue to uplift others in their thoughts and in their actions. Amen!

1

Companionship

Ever thrown a pebble in a pond and watched the ripples it creates? The ripples start off in little circles, but they soon expand and dissipate into the vastness of the water around them, the bigger the splash, the more profound the ripple effect.

Whatever we do, we must think before we do it. In all reality, any action taken by us, whether knowingly or unknowingly, has far reaching consequences. Consequences, which we do not control most of the time! The repercussions of our actions may change lives forever. Just drop a small pebble into a pond of still water and you would know how far reaching the results of that innocent action are.

Human relationships are like the pebbles thrown in the ocean of time we live in. Each relationship creates a ripple effect of its own. True companionship in life is to identify and understand each other's ripples and to have the capability to balance the waves of their emotions settling the agitation in their pond. This companionship is not just limited to our own friends and family, it extends to humanity at large.

Imagine sitting beside an already restless pond contemplating the ripples. You get a tap on your shoulder and this person who you do not know points out to the ripple that you have created. If you were only half a believer, you would surrender to the course nature appoints for you.

Relationships

Sometimes relationships are created
Sometimes they are just made
Sometimes they are given to us
With all their tricks and traits
Sometimes they come like flowers
In colorful prints and shades
Sometimes they lift us up in spirit
For without them life just fades
There are times when we are in them
And times when we are without
If it weren't for relationships
There would be such a drought
As I contemplate relations
I can't help but think of you
For ours is such a special one
And it's all because of you

Ripple Effect

Drop a little pebble into still waters
See the ripples dance away
They move in all directions like concentric circles
A consistent message they indeed display
The ripple effect is far reaching
Impacting everything in its way
Our actions are the pebbles
With repercussions beyond just today
So, stop and think before you act
You might not like what you portray

Coming Together

I couldn't see my reflection
For it was too dark for me to see
The burning of the flame within
Was needed to create the luminosity
There was constant agitation
In a state of uncertainty
It all coming together this way
Induced serenity
There were impediments in my vision
Certain things I couldn't see
Seeing the world through my inner eye
Brought needed clarity
For many have tried to travel
The inner road to connectivity
The more I journey inwards
The closer seems felicity
I know now this relationship
Was always meant to be
For I'm ever thankful to you
For the mercy and generosity

Inner Connection

Who are you
What this life means to you
Look deep into yourself
And you will find the clue
The inner reflection of your thoughts
May tell you something true

Grace

Although I forget, as my heart beats
But your love for me never retreats
My memories fail to reclaim
As if it were an extinguished flame
Yet sometimes it penetrates my soul
A quiver I just can't control
I want to extend out my arm
To try to feel that majestic charm
Against time I forever race
Passion filled, mesmerized by the grace

Destiny's Whisper

Was it the tides of time?
Or the winds of change
That carried me away?
On my high-horse I was
For a while I know
And it felt I'd lost my way
From the high of highs
To the low of lows
My emotions seemed to sway
Had I met you then
When I was incomplete
Would I be who I am today?
What I thought I had lost
The love, the hope, the trust
It all came back that day
Had it not been the void
That I had to fill
Would I yearn for you that way?
And as you held me tight
In your arms that night
Destiny gently whispered, stay

2

Collisions

Every collision in our life forces us to reach conclusions as to why we collided the way we did. We attempt to learn lessons from our collisions as we go along. The new paths we find ourselves on, each time as we collide, almost always are painful and cumbersome in the beginning.

Change requires effort. This effort is translated as pain; pain that we eventually learn to live with and accept as part of our lives. Sometimes change can pose a threat to the present course we are on. The threat slows us down. It creates doubt and confusion. That change in direction, whatever it may be, demands an explanation from us. If we are unable to give ourself one, then we stay suspended. Suspension takes away from us the moments that we can otherwise spend in serving others. Time quietly slips away. Second by second, minute by minute, hour by hour, life that slips away never comes back again.

As time passes by, the same pain becomes a sweet memory

so full of experiences that enables us to grow as individuals. It is these collisions in life that make us who we are today. Had it not been for our collisions of the past, our lives would have not been what they are in the present. For a life without collision, is a life without meaning, and a life so incomplete.

Collisions enable us to shift our perspective a little. Even if it is in the negative direction, we get to see a different pathway. Sometimes it is the worst collisions in our lives that make us see the best horizons.

What I Know Now

For what it seems
With a handful of dreams
Scribbling on blank pages
Riding through life's stages
I have arrived at this place
A journey of varied pace
I know now what I did not know before
What lies ahead I cannot ignore

Neglect

The responsibilities we neglect
As our quests for understanding die
The illusion distorts our vision
And we don't see eye to eye
We get accustomed to the distortion
And we keep on living by
In time we become irrational beings
And our enmities multiply

Superficialities

Creature comforts, luxuries
Entrenched and enthralled
Steady hand, even keel
Steering destiny through it all
Eyes on the goal, focused
Yet we almost always fall
On our knees we seldom get
Unless we have to crawl
Inflated rhetoric full of calculations
Still, we walk right into a wall

Metamorphosis

Cliché as it may sound
It makes the world go round
The circle of life
Entails a lot of strive
And, in its folds
Are countless stories hidden, untold
One doesn't have to look too far
Just leave the door to your heart ajar
And you will see a treasure trove of tales
Inspiring, beguiling, mesmerizing
Gut wrenching, pain inflicting, sobering
Teaching us lessons as they unfold
Chipping away at, chiseling, crafting our perspectives
What seems like a cocoon, opens up eventually
As we flap our wings and fly

The Transcendence

In a trance like the daffodils
As they twirl in the gentle summer breeze
In spite my fallible mediocrities
My agitating universe suddenly is at peace
As I spin, the time stands still
I wish the moments to simply freeze
What my eyes neglect, my heart already believes
There is transcendence in true transformation
Truly, with difficulty comes ease

A Fleeting Moment

Like a flickering candle by the window
Waiting for the wind to blow
Like autumn leaves weak and discolored
Falling to the ground below
Like the moon on a cloudy night
Losing all its glow
We are all here for a fleeting moment
Until it's time for us to go

3

Cobwebs

They look so flimsy, so delicate and so disorganized. Yet they are strong, practical and so skillfully made. They serve the purpose of sustenance for the spider through the simple mode of physical communication, the touch. It is the vibration of the threads of the web that alert the spider of the incoming prey.

We all have personal cobwebs within us. Sometimes we thread our own and sometimes others do it for us. Regardless, we all end up with cobwebs inside of us. These webs, so intricate, so complicated and difficult to understand at times, connect our past to our present and can be extended to weave our future.

How sensitive are the threads to our webs that connect us to our inner self? How much have we spent in mapping our personal webs? Are our webs hampering our ability to shoulder our responsibilities, pulling us down?

Inner Turmoil

The numbness I have in my soul
This state of being, I can no longer ignore
Heedlessness within me
I seldom stand up against and deplore
I march forward to the beat of the drums
Unable to reflect and to explore
Myopic, constricted self-limiting beliefs
My way of life I am programmed to adore
Do I really understand the fundamental necessities?
My connectivity, my dependency, my rapport?
This numbness that I have in my soul
Is a liability I can't live with anymore

The Toll

Tell me where am I headed
And what is my goal?
Do I tend to my whims
Or should I listen to my soul?
When I think I know it all
New realities unfold
The more I ponder reality
The more I relinquish control
Shying away from destiny
Has to have its toll
Tell me where am I headed
And what is my goal?

Forgotten Promises

The waves of my desire
Nudge me astray
And as I stumble and fall
Reason recognizes the disarray
Reflection void of introspection
Is a sign of intellectual decay
When life is in control
Only invincibility we convey
But when disaster stricken
In desperation we obey
The forgotten promises I ignore
As time keeps slipping away

My Creed

The doorstep to my abode
Immovable! Resilient!
Relentlessly trampled upon
In spite of dust and dirt
Still visible and ever shining through
Indifferent to my insolence
Forgiving of my arrogance
Forever hopeful of my return
Waiting for my arrival home

Human Suffering

So in my face, obvious
Yet I don't seem to care
I've become a hollow mold of emptiness
Shallow, and unaware
Like empty vessels, void of empathy
Indifferent to suffering and despair
Introspection is badly needed
To change my state of affair
How can I demand my rights
When my responsibilities, I neglect to bear

Agitation

Fear is being perpetuated
Lies are being told
A chasm has been created
As the narratives unfold
Looming on the horizon
Are symbols, I am told
My inability to understand
Will make me pay the toll
There is a murmur in my heart
Resonating without control
The agitation deep within
Is tearing up my soul

Inner Folds

By reading books we gain knowledge
Yet we hardly spend time knowing our souls
Our thoughts are shaped by externalities
Yet we seldom contemplate what our heart holds
We've reached the limitless skies
Yet we've failed to reach our heart's inner folds

4

Souls

Far too many of us go through our lives without a conscious realization of what it is that we ought to be doing with the intellectual faculties given to us by nature; for indeed we are all endowed with innate capabilities. It is these capabilities that infuse in us a sense of civilization; a sense that enables us to cultivate and educate ourselves, to protect the environment, and to be of service to our fellow beings.

Although we might utilize these faculties to benefit ourselves, mostly our desires for worldly gains, we seldom utilize them for contemplating realms of connectivity for nurturing our souls.

Even more sadly, we hardly ever utilize these intellectual capabilities for maintaining a balance in and around us.

A Soul's Journey

A stroke of fate
A blessing in disguise
You walk away
When I close my eyes
As you drift away
You are no longer constricted
Floating in ecstasy
You are no longer restricted
As reality unveils
Your passion flourishes
Like water quenches
Your longing nourishes
The dawn as it breaks
A light penetrates through
I wake up the next morning
And my heart is full of hue

Signs

Radiating passion, perpetuating serenity
Illuminating the deepest darkest corners of my heart
Unrestricting comfort, captivating charm
Capturing imagination like a magnificent piece of art
Changing perspectives, rejuvenating thoughts
Ever wondered, what all these realities in actuality impart?

The Drowning

I was already drowning
My soul gasping for air
The end was fast approaching
Yet I was unaware
In that fleeting moment
With no time to spare
As I glanced up one last time
He answered my prayer

Hope

I am an anxious soul full of confusion
You being in my life brings me resolution
Like the wind that majestically shapes the sand dunes
You make sway with life's enchanted tunes
And when my worlds come tumbling down
You build me up and wipe away my frown
And when my eyes fill up with tears
You calm me down and erase my fears
As the sunshine is a sign for a brighter day
You lift me up in spirit despite come what may
As the stars twinkle when at night the sky is clear
You bring me courage and my worries disappear

Compassion

Every soul has compassion infused in it, by design
That compassion is a gift, a blessing and a sign
Be mindful of your bounties, wherever you may be
For this skill, is not given to you for free
It's a responsibility you carry till the day you die
If your tongue fails to express it,
It should well up in your eye
For you're only truly compassionate
When you uplift and dignify
Like the raindrop that falls with the intent to give
The seed beneath the soil the love it needs to live
From the seed comes the sapling longing for the light
Every ray of sunshine, aids it in its plight
And as the plant grows, countless flowers bloom
Giving off the fragrance that fills up the room

Due Drops

Like due drops trickling down, glistening every petal
The love is ever present, irrespective of the vessel
Like a murmur it reverberates from within
Like a cool breeze it gently caresses the skin
Tip toeing, effortlessly gliding through
Filling our hearts with a colorful hue

5

Affairs

Without the internal desire to make it happen, people cannot be changed by external stimuli. For a change independent of our internal desire to change, is a cursory change only on an emotional level. Hollow emotions might help us push a ship onto the water but mere 'feelings' cannot chart a course to a specific destination. What good is a ship that just sits on water at the mercy of the waves that might take it wherever they want to?

Like empty vessels we, the masses, aimlessly float on the waves of our emotions. Void of any self-consciousness of true humanistic values or ethical principles, we drift like fallen leaves from one roadside to the other. All the colors turn to a dull shade of brown. Wind blows us around; time disperses us like bits and pieces and when it rains, we simply are cast away to the storm drains like the rest of the dirt on the streets.

A civilized society, given the absence of respect and tolerance for others, is like the endangered species that is rapidly racing towards extinction. We contaminate our social ecosystem with prejudice, racism, and injustice, on one hand, and then turn around and wonder what is happening to our so-called civic world. We pass our verdicts before the court convenes, hanging people prior to conviction. The reins to our future are in the hands of individuals with a materialist lust of this world. These individuals only prowl for infinite power. A power completely void of the true humanistic perspective only soaked in the hunger of selfishness.

This is the time to be looking deep within us. Every individual bears the responsibility to figure out what we have done to be in this depleted state of affairs. It's time to redefine our purpose in this life.

Eye of Desire

To all who believe
You can lead with impulse
Heat recedes exponentially
When flames retire
Your inspirational words may
Beguile a heart or two
But self-corrected action
Is a prerequisite to inspire
Concealed it may be
Your irrationality
Impurities get separated
When exposed to fire
Your outward charm may entice
Sensory stimulation
It is introspective reflection
That induces to aspire
Superficiality is all you may gain
When all is said and done
If you are searching for reality
With the eye of desire

Dichotomy

Dysfunctional dichotomy of greed
Bleeding what's left of our creed
With numb minds we desecrate
We accept, we believe and we perpetuate
Hollow rituals of civilized societies
Norms binding us to distorted realities

A Land of Not So Free

A land is no longer the land of the free
Where opinions become decree
Where pulpits spew hate
Where egos trump humility
Where intolerance creates rigidity
Where you and I can't peacefully disagree

A land can only be the land of the free
Where there is room to just let it be
Where we amicably agree to disagree
Where we show each other mercy
Where I respect you, and you respect me

Unconscious Erosion

Like a cancer, it erodes
Our ability to think straight
Where our experiences act like bait
Shaping the narratives we create
Amplifying our thought patterns
Coding our preferences
Creating unfair references
Influencing the way we think
Predisposing us to fallacies
That we unconsciously entertain
Without knowing that it constrains
Our ability to be openminded

Humble Stare

Crushed in a moment
Were all their hopes and dreams
Vanished from their faces
Were their radiant gleams
Solemn was the moment
Reflective was the mood
When the wild winds of detestation
Destroyed their neighborhood
Trickling down their cheeks
Was a stream of tears
Reflecting in their eyes
Were a lot of fears
Rising to the sky
Was a humble stare
Echoing through the space
Was a silent prayer
Guide the intolerant
Remove our despair
Send us down some mercy
That we may start to care

The Abyss

We stand at the cliff, edging towards the abyss
Destroying our way of life, searching for bliss
Startled by our inability to comprehend
Unable to see the damage and to amend
Intoxicated with extravagance, programmed to consume
Devouring the planet, to our inevitable doom
Pillaging, ravaging, polluting our home
Unreflective of the root cause of all we bemoan
Clinging to a rhetoric steeped in greed
We are poised to destroy the human creed
Living in a state of heedlessness it seems
Where equity and justice are no longer the dreams
Locked up we are in demented realities
Wonder who, we are trying to appease
Aren't we supposed to be dignified and elevated?
Stewards of this planet, mindful and calculated?
Our leaders get enriched at the expense of the public
Our society, a banana republic
Misguided are our loyalties, our sense of ethics a joke
The rich amass wealth on the backs of working folk
What oxygen is to blood, introspection is to thought
When there is no reasoning, the character starts to rot

6

Thoughts

One man's thoughts are another man's fuel for more thoughts. For thoughts are induced to justify our actions. And actions are caused by what we think! Now isn't that a strange predicament?

Sometimes we need to take ourselves out of that loop and look at things from a different perspective. Paradigm shifts are key to evaluating situations that require lifechanging decisions. But a shift in perspectives requires a change in our thought process. Too often change is perceived as pain. Even when change may be for the better. It is the fear of pain that stops us from acting and prompts us to analyze. Too much analysis can bring us confusion and the inability to progress in the positive direction.

A positive direction is not necessarily a dedicated path in one direction. It is indeed a movement in all directions. Only when we grow in all directions equally, we tend to grasp the true essence of who we are and what we can become.

I Swear

Floating on the water
Gliding through the air
It was always meant to be
But I was unaware
Soothing to my soul
Was a silent prayer
Dew laden petals
Spring was everywhere
It was a fleeting moment
When I caught your stare
Tranquility transcended deep within
My heart wanted to share
The flame got ignited that day
And so began our affair

Out in the Open

Until today you were only in my heart
But now you are out in the open
Why did I let you loose, out there?
Why did I let go of my feelings?
I guess my love for you has grown
Above and beyond me
I had to let go!
I had to turn it loose!

Slow Trickles

What is it that is trickling?
Trickling from up above
Soaked in nothing but love
Seeping into every hole
Nourishing the human soul
What is it that is trickling?
Calling you and me
Setting our hearts free
Stroking our inner desires
Burning passionate fires
What is it that is trickling?

Your Awareness

The awareness of my love for you
Is a constant simmering thought
Gushing through my veins
Pumping in my heart
Stimulating my sense of perception
Like a beautiful piece of art
Calming, like a gentle summer breeze
Putting my internal agitation at ease
Slowly caressing my skin
Like a whirling dervish I spin
Free from the shackles of time
Floating perpetually in space
Within me and outside of me
In my grasp and beyond me
The awareness of my love for you
Is a constant simmering thought

7

Oaths

Educators take the Socratic Oath. Doctors take the Hippocratic Oath. Public servants take the Oath of Office. If oaths were taken seriously by people, we would have had a perfectly accountable system. Thoughtless oaths create selfish accountabilities where the intentions are to work for our own personal gains at any cost.

What if there was a tool that could decipher the intent of our hearts? What if there was a 'conscience meter' that we could hook up to people to see whether they really are sincere, like a lie detector?

But as I thought of it some more, I realized that our intentions are manifested in our actions; for what we conceive internally we often manifest externally. What we think is how we behave when we think no one is looking. But if we realize that we are constantly being watched, then I doubt anyone of us would dare act inappropriately, in defiance of the oaths that we so ceremoniously take in our personal or public discourses. And if we did slip up, we would show signs of remorse and accept the consequences.

Promises

The promises we made
When we said that we would
The pacts we created
With the hands that we shook
The hopes we raised
With the pledges that we took
The emotions that we stirred
With our vows for brotherhood
Aren't all these written
As oaths in the book?

Getting By

Every morning I get up
And I deal with the hand
That is dealt by you
How many times
Do I pretend to know it all
When I haven't got a clue
Weakened in my resolve
When I fail to see it all
With my limited point of view
Patient I have to be
As I stumble and fall
And I will get through

Good Deeds

Deeds that I fail to carry on
From the thoughts that come my way
My priorities lie elsewhere
So my passion leads me astray
The promises I break knowingly
I will regret one day
Sometimes we get it effortlessly
Sometimes we learn the hard way
We must continuously perform good deeds
As time does tend to slip away

Our Backdoor

In our quest to explore the cosmos
Like we've never done before
I wish we fall in love again
With our own backdoor
For the treasures it offers us
Both life giving and life saving
Are awe inspiring too!
As we race to observe the universe
And in its vastness, we immerse
Let us also recognize and respect
The oath we take as stewards
The Earth that continues to cradle us
Needs reverence too!

8

Consciousness

Our consciousness predates our physical being and will outlast its demise. It is the essence that connects our souls to that which is the reality of all realities. Unfortunately, far too many of us, on a daily basis, continue to fall from grace because of our inability to avail our consciousness for what it was designed for. The reason for that failure is our inability to channel our desires from the exterior to that which is the interior – our self.

Actions are by intentions, make no mistake about it. Our behavior is an active manifestation of our inner desires. And more often than not, we tend to preface our actions with our rhetoric. The words that come out of us, the thoughts that provoke us and the imagination that fuels us, need self-analysis perpetually.

For it is our imagination, infested with a lust to feed our low base desires, which manifests in our intentions first followed with our actions. And when our intentions are tainted with self-interest rather than self-analysis, we deviate from the path. This deviation is a sign of weakness in our ability to rein in the influence our desires exert on our psyche at all times.

Cancer

Here I go again dancing with the shadows of my desire
Soaked in a passion fueled with corrupt imagination
Tangled in a web of sensory paraphernalia
I have lost my ability to analyze my intentions
Flowing freely inside of me are my needs
Needs that cling to me like a cancerous disease
Invading every cell of my conscience
Making me weak and vulnerable to influences
My shadows take the best of me
As I dance with them so intimately

Words

Words when like spears
They perpetuate fears
Crippling our senses
Rendering us defenseless
Numbing, damaging, intoxicating
Debilitating, capturing, encapsulating
Words when like tears
Cleanse and clears
Influencing our goals
Uplifting our souls
Mesmerizing, tantalizing, captivating
Awe inspiring, hope infusing, life giving

Salesman

Illusion prone in need of clarity
A flawless pitch, but lacking sincerity
Advancing ideas of grandiose schemes
Empty promises, packed with dreams
Crafting clever messages to feed the need
With only one motivation; greed
There is a salesman inside every personality
The trick is to stay away from selling superficiality

Beckoning

In the vestibules of imagination tucked away
Implanted deep in the crevices of my soul
Flickering, fluttering, glimmering
The hope that makes me whole
Perpetuating through time, echoing in space
Beckoning endlessly for that embrace
Awe inspiring, overwhelming, humbling
Calling me softly with grace

The Coming of Age

The coming of age!
Beckons me to turn a new page
But the page doesn't turn
Because I seldom learn
From what life teaches me, preaches me
Clinging on to the past, yet I cast
A glance in the future and what it holds
How many of my dreams have I sold?

The coming of age!
It forces me to be a sage
Flaunting my wisdom
Contrived from a broken system
Thinking I'm the only one who knows
Just because life has given me a few blows
But do I reflect, do I understand
The decree of nature as it plays its hand?

The coming of age!
The crescendo of rage
My inability to assuage
The agitation that runs deep
Got to wake up from this deep sleep
As the climb is still very steep
There is a world that lies ahead of me
How should I let go and let it be?

ABRAR ANSARI

The coming of age!
Breaking free of the bondage
Why be shackled up in a cage
Like an eagle, there has to be flight
Like a warrior, I must fight
For as long as I live, I should thrive
To my heart's tunes, I must jive
Cause I'm alive…I'm alive…I'm alive!

9

Interdependencies

There is an intricate relationship between the esoteric and the exoteric. It's symbiotic! To understand the ebbs and flows of the physical universe, one must also learn a thing or two about traversing the meta-physical realm. Until we see the interconnectivity between the two, we can't learn to solve today's complex social, environmental, and economic problems.

Defining the significance of our existence in this vast universe, without recognizing our interconnectivity, with the bigger universe, is an exercise in futility.

Such are the interdependencies of human consciousness with the universe around us. Our conscious defines the universe, and the universe defines it.

Who Am I?

Don't take away my individuality
It's proof of my independence
It's a product of my thoughts
The basis of my transcendence
An element of my uniqueness
A source of my dependence
A face to my emotions
Identifier of my existence

Connectivity

I connect to you
You connect to me
Us connecting with many
Creates connectivity
I believe in you
You believe in me
Us believing in many
Creates veracity
I soothing you
You soothing me
Us soothing many
Creates harmony
I trusting you
You trusting me
Us trusting in many
Creates humanity

Mother

Present in my eyes is your reflection
That shines through perpetually
Embedded in my psyche are your thoughts
That influence my actions
Gushing through my veins is your essence
That is the fabric of my being
It is you who has carried me painstakingly
When I was the most vulnerable
For indeed you are a gift of mercy
An awe-inspiring creation of the most merciful

10

Destiny

There comes a time in every man's life when he feels like a vessel floating on the ocean in the hope of finding land. With sails spread and the course charted, all hopes hinge on those favorable winds to pick up. The winds do pick up, gently pushing the vessel forward. After what seems like days of endless sailing, land is sighted. The eyes are drawn towards this piece of land not because she is beautiful, for indeed she is; not because the sun gleams on her making her smile back at you, indeed that is the case; not because her warmth is radiating and one feels like basking in it, indeed that is the case; but because to go anywhere else just does not make any sense. All signs point towards her, even the north-star twinkles as it peaks momentarily from behind the lonely cloud on a moon-lit night. She becomes your destiny; one that beckons to you calling out your name, reminding you to cease the moment. For she is a blessing not to be taken for granted but to be accepted with awe and humility.

Sublime Contemplation

I was a boat on water yearning for land
Winds gusting forward, wild waves in command
At the mercy of the environment
The course so it seemed charted
The hope in me departed
As into the night I sailed
It seemed in life, I have failed
I had no strength to fight
To let go felt right

But the sun came up at dawn
The water calm, the winds gone
Clenched in my palms I could feel the sand
To my surprise I was on land
All that turmoil, so it may seem
Washed away like an unpleasant dream
What started with temporal agitation
Has given birth to sublime contemplation
I embrace her as my destiny
With reverence and with humility

One Droplet at a Time

Submerged in your essence
One droplet at a time
Emerged from this union
A journey so sublime
I didn't have the foresight to see
The path I took, will bring you to me
Now I see, what it's meant to be
A journey together of tranquility
Like a mirage it was meaningless
An abode so full of emptiness
Now filled with your compassion
I am drenched in your passion
With you contentment I have found
My thoughts no longer confound
I confess my love with openness
What I feel cannot be suppressed
Your signs are the inspiration
My thoughts need for reflection
A ray of continuous mercy
A source for affection
Submerged in your essence
One droplet at a time
Emerged from this union
A journey so sublime

Smile

Smile for you have a beautiful one
Smile and your wrongs may be undone
Smile will spread happiness
Smile takes away the weariness
Smile in the morning gracefully
Smile just once but endlessly
Smile with your heart
Smile with your soul
Smile is something you control
Smile when you're feeling down
Smile even when you want to frown
Smile in the face of agony
Smile it will end your misery
Smile for it makes me smile

ABOUT THE AUTHOR

Abrar was a poet long before he became an author, a mentor, a coach and a management consultant. He is the co-founder of Abstract Space Inc., a boutique management consultancy, and the founder of the Management by INTENT business transformation frameworks.

Abrar is passionate about responsible, intent-driven leadership that is dedicated to the cause of creating balance and harmony. This means preserving, supporting, and nurturing the human-side of business, enabling leaders to better understand their organization's true impact and to realign to a higher purpose for catering to the needs of all their stakeholders.

Abrar's ability to connect with you on an individual basis as well as connect with groups, large and small, gives him an edge when he asks others to take a moment to think.

For more info, visit: www.managementbyintent.com

www.ingramcontent.com/pod-product-compliance
Lightning Source LLC
Chambersburg PA
CBHW070323120526
44590CB00017B/2795